PIANO · VOCAL · GUITAR

ELTON JOHN
Ballads

P9-DYX-833

This book was purchased
with funds from the
New Book Endowment
of The Library Foundation.

For more information
on charitable giving
opportunities to benefit
The Library, including
a gift through your will,
please contact:
The Library Foundation
301 York Street
Louisville, KY 40203-2257
502/574-1654

ISBN 0-7935-3350-3

HAL·LEONARD®
CORPORATION
7777 W. BLUEMOUND RD. P.O. BOX 13819 MILWAUKEE, WI 53213

ELTON JOHN
Ballads

CONTENTS

BLUE EYES

Words and Music by ELTON JOHN
and GARY OSBORNE

BORDER SONG

Words and Music by ELTON JOHN
and BERNIE TAUPIN

Slowly, with a beat

8

CANDLE IN THE WIND

Music by ELTON JOHN
Words by BERNIE TAUPIN

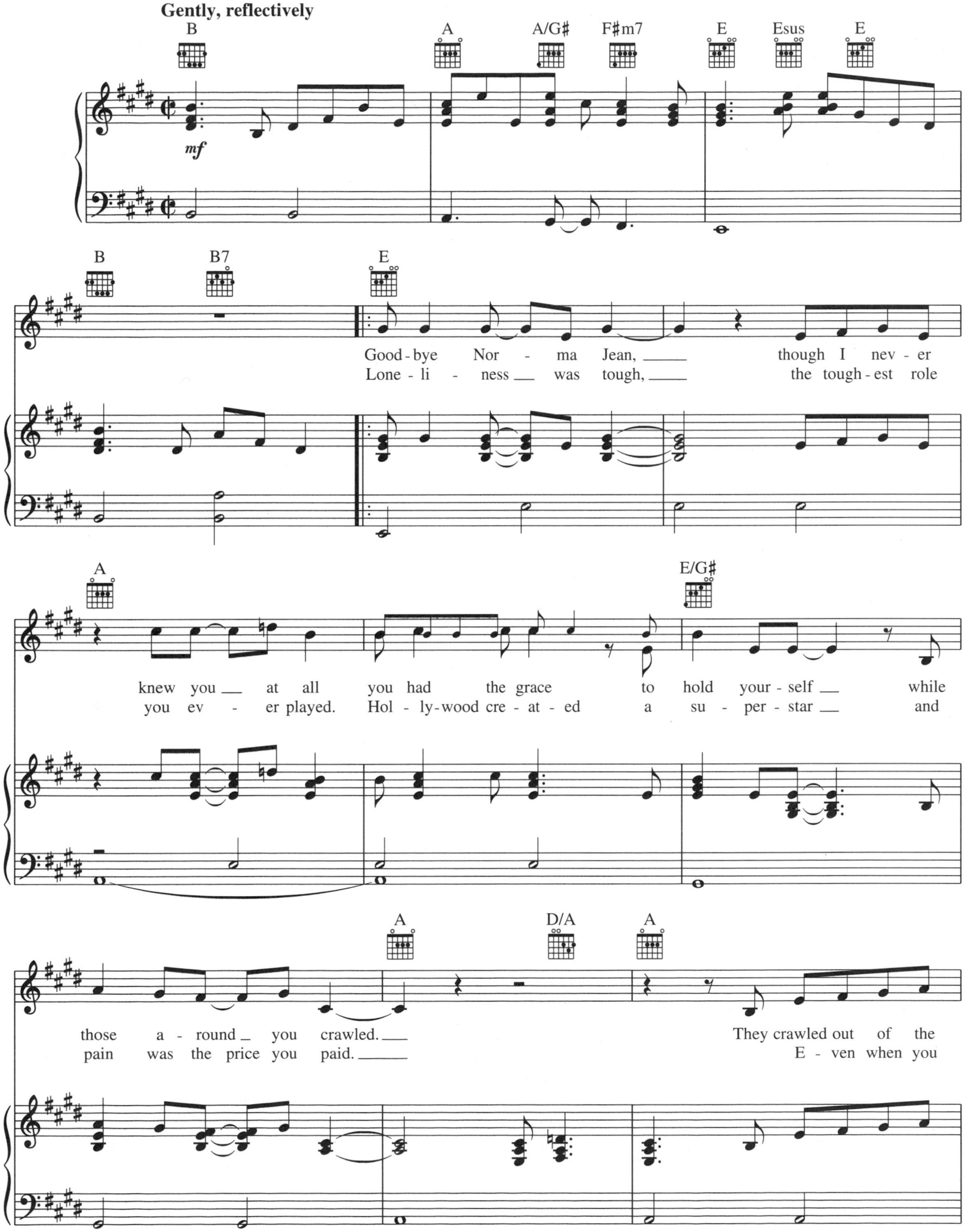
Gently, reflectively
B
A
A/G#
F#m7
E
Esus
E
mf
B
B7
E
Good-bye Nor - ma Jean, ___ though I nev - er
Lone - li - ness ___ was tough, ___ the tough - est role
A
E/G#
knew you ___ at all you had the grace to hold your - self ___ while
you ev - er played. Hol - ly-wood cre - at - ed a su - per - star ___ and
A
D/A
A
those a - round ___ you crawled. ___ They crawled out of the
pain was the price you paid. ___ E - ven when you

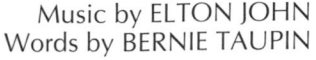

Good-bye Nor-ma Jean, from a young man in the

twen-ty sec-ond row ___ who sees you as some-thing more than sex-ual, ___ more than

just our Mar-i-lyn Mon-roe.   It

seems to me ___ you lived ___ your life ___ like a can-dle in ___ the wind, ___

CHLOE

Words and Music by ELTON JOHN
and GARY OSBORNE

Moderately slow, in 2

How come you're so un - der - stand - in'
How you han - dle what you live through
You're the life - line that I cling to

when I tell you all my lies,
I can nev - er hope to learn,
when I feel like giv - in' in,

DANIEL

Words and Music by ELTON JOHN
and BERNIE TAUPIN

Moderately bright

1.4. Dan - iel is trav - 'ling to - night___ on a plane ___
2. They say Spain is pret - ty 'though I've nev - er been ___
3. *Instrumental ad lib. at 1st D.S. (small notes)*

I can see the red ___ tail - lights ___
Well Dan - iel says ___ it's the best place ___ he's

23

DON'T LET THE SUN GO DOWN ON ME

Words and Music by ELTON JOHN
and BERNIE TAUPIN

I can't_ light no more of your dark - ness.

All my pic - tures _____ seem to fade_ to black_ and white. _

EMPTY GARDEN
(HEY HEY JOHNNY)

Words and Music by ELTON JOHN
and BERNIE TAUPIN

What hap-pened here?___ As the
New York sun-set dis-ap-peared___ I found an Emp-ty Gar - den___
a-mong the flag-stones there.___ Who___ lived___ here?___ He
must have been a gar-den-er who cared a lot,___ who weed-ed out the tears and grew a

FRIENDS

Words and Music by ELTON JOHN
and BERNIE TAUPIN

GOODBYE YELLOW BRICK ROAD

Words and Music by ELTON JOHN
and BERNIE TAUPIN

Moderately slow, in 2

When are you gon-na come down When are you going to land
What do you think you'll do then I bet that -'ll shoot down ___ your plane

___ I should have stayed ___ on the farm ___ Should have list - ened ___ to my ___ old man
It -'ll take you a cou - ple of vod - ka and ton - ics to set you on your feet a - gain

___ You know you can't hold ___ me for - ev - er ___ I did - n't sign up ___ with you ___
May - be you'll get ___ a re - place - ment ___ there's plen - ty like me to be found

39

MONA LISAS AND MAD HATTERS

Words and Music by ELTON JOHN
and BERNIE TAUPIN

THE LAST SONG

Words and Music by ELTON JOHN
and BERNIE TAUPIN

Am

shake   this an - ger?   I need your gen - tle hands _   to
things that were nev - er spo - ken. That kind of un - der - stand - ing

G

G7   **C**

keep   me   calm. __   'Cause I   nev - er thought _ I'd lose. __   I
sets   me   free. __

rall.   *a tempo*

G/B   **Am**

on - ly thought _ I'd win. __   I   nev - er dreamed _ I'd feel __   this fire _

G   **F**

__ be-neath my skin.   I can't be - lieve you   love __ me.   I nev - er thought you'd

LEVON

Words and Music by ELTON JOHN
and BERNIE TAUPIN

Bb   **F/A**   **Gm7**   **F**

Christ-mas day____ when the New York Times__ said God____ is dead____ and__ war's be - gun.____

Bb   **F/A**   **Gm7**

Guitar Tacet

Al-vin Tos-tig has__ a son__ to-day._____   And he shall__ be Le -

Bb   **F/A**

- von.   And he shall__ be a good____ man.____   And he shall__ be__ Le -

Bb   **F/A**

- von ____ in tra - di - tion with the fam - 'ly plan____ and he shall__ be__ Le -

NIKITA

Words and Music by ELTON JOHN
and BERNIE TAUPIN

Hey, Nik - it - a, is it cold in your lit - tle corn - er
Do you ev - er dream of me? Do you ev - er see the let - ters

of the world? You could roll a - round the globe,
that I write? When you look up through the wire,

09

THE ONE

Words and Music by ELTON JOHN
and BERNIE TAUPIN

I saw you danc - in' out __ the o - cean, __
There are car - a - vans __ we fol - low, __

ROCKET MAN
(I THINK IT'S GONNA BE A LONG LONG TIME)

Moderately slow, with a beat

Words and Music by ELTON JOHN
and BERNIE TAUPIN

She packed_ my bags_ last night pre-flight,___ Ze-ro hour_ Nine A.M.___ And I'm gon-na be high ___ as a kite by then. I miss_ the earth_ so much_ I miss my wife,___ it's lone-ly out_ in space.___

SACRIFICE

Words and Music by ELTON JOHN
and BERNIE TAUPIN

1
F(add9)
F/G
2
F(add9)
C
F
Dm7
G
C
F
Dm7
G
D.S. al Coda
Cold, _ cold heart _
CODA
C
F
Dm
G
No sac - ri - fice ___ at all.
C
F
Dm
G
Repeat and Fade
No sac - ri - fice ___ at all.

SOMEONE SAVED MY LIFE TONIGHT

Words and Music by ELTON JOHN
and BERNIE TAUPIN

Verse 2. I never realized the passing hours
        Of evening showers,
        A slip noose hanging in my darkest dreams.
        I'm strangled by your haunted social scene
        Just a pawn out-played by a dominating queen.
        It's four-o-clock in the morning
        Damn it!
        Listen to me good.
        I'm sleeping with myself tonight
        Saved in time, thank God my music's still alive.
      To Chorus

SORRY SEEMS TO BE THE HARDEST WORD

Words and Music by ELTON JOHN
and BERNIE TAUPIN

Slow lament

TINY DANCER

Words and Music by ELTON JOHN
and BERNIE TAUPIN

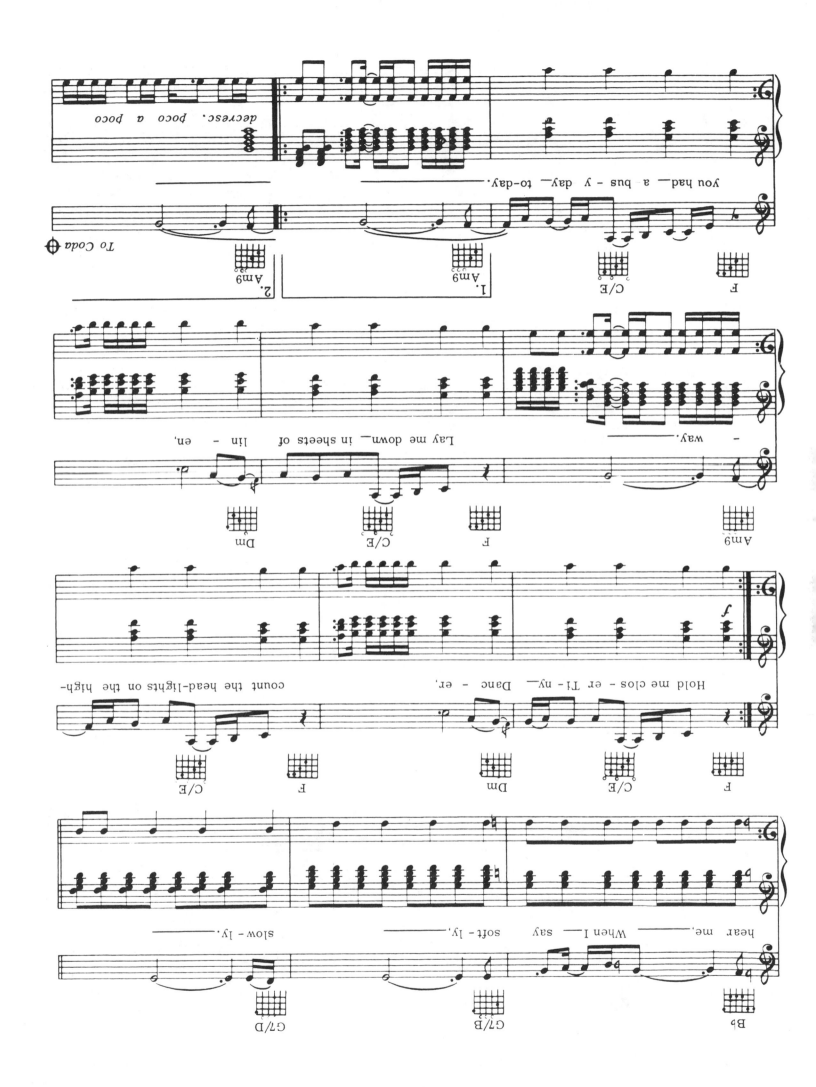

YOU GOTTA LOVE SOMEONE

(Featured In The Motion Picture "DAYS OF THUNDER")

Words and Music by ELTON JOHN
and BERNIE TAUPIN

91

YOUR SONG

Words and Music by ELTON JOHN
and BERNIE TAUPIN